EDGE
BOOKS™

INFECTED!

MALARIA

HOW A PARASITE CHANGED HISTORY

by Jeanne Marie Ford

Consultant

David Sullivan, MD
Professor of Molecular Microbiology and Immunology
Johns Hopkins Bloomberg School of Public Health

CAPSTONE PRESS
a capstone imprint

Edge Books are published by Capstone Press,
1710 Roe Crest Drive, North Mankato, Minnesota 56003
www.mycapstone.com

Library of Congress Cataloging-in-Publication Data
Names: Ford, Jeanne Marie, 1971- author.
Title: Malaria : how a parasite changed history / by Jeanne Marie Ford.
Description: North Mankato, Minnesota : Capstone Press, [2019] | Series:
  Infected! | "Edge Books are published by Capstone Press." | Audience: Ages
  8-14. | Audience: Grades 7 to 8. | Includes bibliographical references and
  index.
Identifiers: LCCN 2018036905 (print) | LCCN 2018037290 (ebook) | ISBN
  9781543555158 (ebook) | ISBN 9781543555059 (hardcover : alk. paper)
Subjects: LCSH: Malaria--Juvenile literature. | Malaria--Prevention--Juvenile
  literature. | Diseases and history--Juvenile literature. | Mosquitoes as
  carriers of disease--Juvenile literature.
Classification: LCC RC157 (ebook) | LCC RC157 .F67 2019 (print) | DDC
  616.9/362--dc23
LC record available at https://lccn.loc.gov/2018036905

Editorial Credits
Editor: Maddie Spalding
Designer: Craig Hinton
Production Specialist: Ryan Gale

Quote Sources
p. 9, Donald McRae, "Anyika Onuora: The Untold Story of Britain's Rio Olympic Medal Winner Who Nearly Died." *Guardian*, April 24, 2017; p. 29, Chimamanda Ngozi Adichie, "Chimamanda Ngozi Adichie on Growing Up Surrounded by Malaria." *Evening Standard*, April 25, 2018

Photo Credits
Getty Images, Kevin Frayer, cover (scientist); National Institute of Health: U.S. National Library of Medicine, 16–17; Newscom: Andy Astfalck/NurPhoto/Sipa USA, 4–5, Chine Nouvelle/SIPA, 13, 26, Stoyan Nenov/Reuters, 9; President's Malaria Initiative: Alison Bird/PMI, 25, Brant Stewart/RTI, 24; Science Source: CDC, 22–23; Shutterstock Images: Airin.dizain, cover (mosquito), Belenos, 10, bolarzeal, 7, Everett Historical, 21, Jamikorn Sooktaramorn, 15, Kletr, 6, toeytoey, 18; USAID: USAID/ Liberia, 29

Design Elements
Shutterstock Images: ilolab

Printed in the United States of America.
PA48

TABLE OF CONTENTS

CHAPTER 1

SURVIVING MALARIA

In October 2015 world-class sprinter Anyika Onuora huddled under the covers in her apartment in England. Her body shook with chills. Minutes later she felt hot. She was drenched in sweat. She knew something was very wrong.

Onuora's phone rang. It was her doctor. He had test results on the samples she had given the day before. He told her the test results. He found that there was a problem with her kidneys. He told her to see a doctor in London who could **diagnose** and treat her.

Onuora could not find anyone to drive her to the hospital. So she drove herself. She collapsed when she reached the hospital's reception desk.

diagnose—to find the cause of a problem

Her head swam with dizziness. She was afraid she was going to die.

Doctors ordered tests and scans. Finally, they reached a diagnosis: malaria.

Sprinter Anyika Onuora was training for the 2016 Olympic Games before she got malaria.

Certain types of mosquitoes pass along malaria when they bite people.

MALARIA'S EFFECTS

Certain types of mosquitoes carry the malaria parasite. Today mosquitoes that carry malaria live mainly in **tropical** areas. This includes most countries in Africa. A **parasite** causes this disease. The parasite is a tiny **organism**. It infects a mosquito. A mosquito then bites people and drinks their blood. This passes the parasite on to humans.

Onuora had recently visited her father's home village in Nigeria. While there she had taken medication to prevent malaria. But she still got the disease.

tropical—having a hot and humid climate
parasite—a living thing that lives off another living thing, such as an animal or human
organism—a living thing that is made up of one or more cells

There are four different types of malaria parasites. They cause different **symptoms**. Some parasites are deadlier than others. Onuora had been infected with the most life-threatening malaria parasite. It can cause kidneys or other organs to fail. Onuora needed to be treated right away.

In the hospital Onuora's body temperature climbed. A nurse packed bags of ice around her. The ice helped cool Onuora.

Doctors gave Onuora medicine through an IV bag. The medicine dripped from the bag into her veins. Doctors told her she would have died if she had waited any longer to seek treatment.

symptom—a change in a person's body or mind that is a sign of a disease

Malaria is most common in tropical nations, such as Nigeria.

Onuora focused on getting healthy again so she could compete in the 2016 Summer Olympic Games. She had been training for this event for years. Onuora was one of Great Britain's best sprinters. She had been favored to win a medal. Now she was too weak to walk.

OLYMPIC DREAMS

Onuora gradually began to feel stronger as the medicine healed her. She did walking drills to strengthen her muscles. She took laps around the hospital hallways with her IV pole.

Onuora finally went home from the hospital in late October. She jogged a few steps. She began to feel well again. She gradually increased her distance and speed. By the next summer, she was chosen to be on a relay team in the 2016 Summer Olympics. Her team won a bronze medal. Onuora cried as she clutched her medal. She had fought hard to earn it.

Onuora used her Olympic fame to raise awareness about malaria. "It [malaria] can happen to anyone—and be overcome," she said in an interview in 2017. "I did it. And it really feels like a fantastic achievement."

Anyika Onuora (right) stands with her relay team after winning a bronze medal at the 2016 Summer Olympics.

CHAPTER 2

MALARIA'S EARLY HISTORY

Malaria is one of the oldest known human diseases. Chinese doctors first described its symptoms of fever, aches, and pains in 2700 BC. Malaria **epidemics** caused many deaths across the ancient world.

Today people can explore Rome and learn how malaria killed many people in the ancient city.

epidemic—an outbreak of a disease that affects many people within a particular region

About 2,000 years ago, Chinese people used herbal medicines to treat malaria symptoms, such as fever. Some treatments worked better than others. One treatment that helped used a plant called sweet wormwood. These medicines remained mostly unknown outside of China. They would later be lost to history for centuries.

MALARIA AND THE ROMAN EMPIRE

The Roman Empire was one of the largest empires in history. It collapsed in AD 476. This was partially because of failed crops and foreign invaders. Today scientists believe that malaria also played a key role. In 2016 researchers examined bones from three Roman graves. They found evidence of the parasite that causes malaria. They believe that the disease spread from Africa to Italy as the Roman Empire expanded. An epidemic may have killed large numbers of Romans. Their deaths probably contributed to the fall of the Roman Empire.

QUININE

Europeans and the African people they enslaved settled in North and South America in the 1500s. Some of these settlers had been infected with malaria. Mosquitoes quickly began to spread the disease to other people.

In the 1600s Native Americans in Peru discovered a treatment for malaria. They ground the bark of a tree called cinchona into a powder. They dissolved it in wine and drank it. Settlers took this knowledge back to Europe.

In the 1820s two European scientists found the malaria-fighting chemical in cinchona bark. They used it to make a drug called quinine. They soon discovered that quinine could be used both to treat and prevent malaria.

Many researchers believe that quinine helped European armies conquer tropical areas in Asia and Africa. Native people in these regions did not have these treatments. They were more likely than the European settlers to get malaria and die from the disease.

Today people still make quinine from cinchona bark to treat malaria.

FAST FACT

Quinine tastes bitter. It was often made into a powder and mixed into other substances to make it easier to drink. Tonic water, which contains quinine, is still sold today.

CHAPTER 3

FINDING A CAUSE

The cause of malaria remained a mystery for thousands of years. People living in the Middle Eastern city of Babylon between 2300 BC and AD 1000 blamed malaria on an angry god. Other ancient cultures had different ideas. In about 600 BC people in India thought insect bites caused malaria. Ancient Romans believed foul-smelling air from a swamp or marsh caused malaria. They called this bad air miasma.

SCIENTIFIC DISCOVERIES

The miasma **theory** remained popular for centuries. But by the late 1800s, many scientists began to think that mosquitoes **transmitted** malaria. Mosquitoes bred in hot swamps or coastal areas where malaria was most common.

theory—an idea or set of ideas that scientists use to explain something
transmit—to pass on something from one organism to another

Doctors began to perform **autopsies** on patients who had died of malaria. They discovered black specks in the patients' blood. The patients' organs had turned black. The doctors realized that malaria moved through a person's bloodstream.

Some people in the ancient world believed malaria came from swamps or marshes.

autopsy—an examination of a dead person's body that helps determine the cause of death

In 1880 a French doctor named Alphonse Laveran saw something unusual in the blood of a malaria patient. It was a parasite, and it was moving.

English researcher Ronald Ross believed that the parasite probably lived inside a certain type of mosquito. He examined thousands of mosquitoes under a microscope. A type of mosquito with spotted wings had black specks in its stomach. This type of mosquito was the *Anopheles* mosquito. It was the carrier of the malaria parasite. The black specks came from the parasite.

In 1898 Italian scientist Giovanni Grassi experimented with *Anopheles* mosquitoes in Rome. He found a man who agreed to be bitten by mosquitoes. These mosquitoes had fed on the blood of malaria patients. The man soon came down with the disease. But malaria was common in Rome at that time. Scientists could not be certain that mosquitoes had caused his illness.

Doctor Alphonse Laveran received a Nobel Prize in 1907 for his medical discoveries.

Italian researchers contacted another scientist named Patrick Manson. Manson lived in London. There were no malaria outbreaks in London. The Italian researchers shipped infected mosquitoes to Manson. Manson's son volunteered to let them bite him. He came down with malaria, which Manson treated with quinine. This experiment confirmed that the *Anopheles* mosquito transmitted malaria.

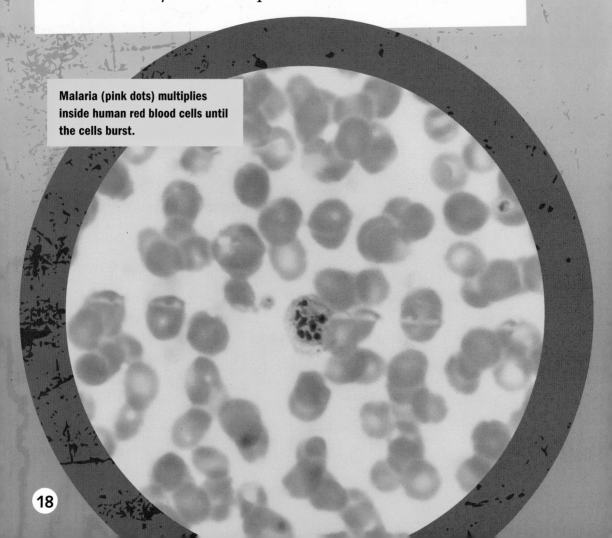

Malaria (pink dots) multiplies inside human red blood cells until the cells burst.

THE MALARIA CYCLE

Only certain species of female *Anopheles* mosquitoes transmit malaria. Mosquitoes spit out saliva when they bite. Then the malaria parasite enters a person's bloodstream. The parasite multiplies in the liver. Then it moves throughout the bloodstream. It infects a person's red blood cells. Red blood cells contain a protein that carries oxygen throughout a person's body. The parasite feeds on this protein. This leaves behind a waste product. The waste product causes the black color seen in a malaria patient's organs.

When a mosquito bites an infected human, the parasite is transmitted to the mosquito. The mosquito carries the parasite to the next person it bites. The cycle of infection continues.

CHAPTER 4

FIGHTING MALARIA

Scientists discovered the cause of malaria during the 1880s. Then their focus turned to finding new treatments. Throughout the 1900s people developed different ways to treat and prevent malaria.

THE PANAMA CANAL

In 1904 American workers began building a canal in Panama. But many workers soon began dying from malaria. Doctors took swift action. They made a plan to reduce the number of mosquitoes in the area. They drained water from swamps where mosquitoes bred. They also cut brush and grass where mosquitoes lived. They used chemicals such as sulfur to kill mosquitoes and their eggs.

Doctors also gave workers quinine powder to prevent malaria. Infection rates dropped. Thousands of lives were likely saved because of these measures.

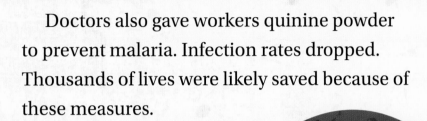

Malaria became widespread among workers who helped build the Panama Canal in the early 1900s.

FAST FACT

The mosquito is the world's deadliest animal. It spreads many diseases. Malaria kills more people than any other illness transmitted by mosquitoes.

WORLD WAR II

Many battles in World War II (1939–1945) were fought in tropical areas such as the South Pacific. Quinine shortages threatened troops' lives. Preventing and curing malaria became important to the war effort. Scientists developed a drug called chloroquine. This drug was similar to quinine.

In the 1940s and 1950s planes sometimes sprayed DDT over marshy areas in the United States.

Scientists also developed a chemical called DDT. This chemical killed disease-carrying insects. Soldiers sprayed it in areas where mosquitoes bred.

After World War II, the U.S. Communicable Disease Center and the World Health Organization (WHO) continued to fight malaria. The disease was eliminated from the United States in 1951. In 1955 the WHO announced its goal to **eradicate** malaria worldwide.

eradicate—to completely eliminate something, such as a disease

CHAPTER 5

TREATING MALARIA

The global effort to eradicate malaria produced exciting results in its first years. The rate of infection dropped in many places. But in Africa the efforts were not as successful. Poverty prevented many people from receiving quality health care.

Workers in Kenya prepare to spray homes with insecticide to kill disease-carrying mosquitoes.

In the late 1950s some malaria parasites became **resistant** to chloroquine. In 1969 the WHO gave up on its effort to eradicate the disease worldwide. Funding for malaria research shrank.

In 1972 DDT was banned in the United States. It was found to harm the environment. It can cause diseases such as cancer. Still, some countries continued to use DDT to fight malaria.

In the 1980s and 1990s mosquitoes became resistant to DDT. Malaria began to make a comeback in areas where it once had been controlled.

Mosquito nets are an inexpensive way to help prevent malaria.

resistant—no longer affected by a chemical or a drug

A NEW DRUG

Around the same time, the Chinese government began searching for new malaria treatments. Scientist Tu Youyou took charge of the research in 1969. She and her team studied ancient Chinese texts to find malaria medicines. They tested hundreds of herbs on mice infected with the malaria parasite. One herb worked to kill the parasites. It came from a plant called sweet wormwood. Tu used ancient recipes to remove chemicals from the plants. She found one chemical called artemisinin. It was 100 percent effective in killing the malaria parasite.

FAST FACT

The ancient Chinese text that Tu Youyou studied was about 1,600 years old.

Chinese scientist Tu Youyou devoted much of her career to developing artemisinin treatments for malaria.

SICKLE CELL DISEASE

Sickle cell disease is a serious blood disorder. Scientists discovered that people with the sickle cell gene most commonly come from the areas of Africa that are hit hardest by malaria. The sickle cell gene helps protect people from severe malaria disease. But people with sickle cell disease must deal with the painful and sometimes deadly symptoms caused by the disease. Symptoms of sickle cell disease include severe pain and shortness of breath.

Because of the Chinese government's secrecy, other countries did not learn about Tu's discovery for many years. Today drugs made with artemisinin are the most effective treatments available for malaria.

FUTURE RESEARCH

Artemisinin drugs save more than 1 million people each year. But recently these drugs have been less effective against malaria parasites. The drugs are taking longer to get rid of the parasite in a person's body. Researchers are working on new drugs. They are also developing new and safer chemicals to kill insects.

gene—the part of a cell that controls the traits passed down from parents to their children

Scientists began testing a **vaccine** for malaria in 2009. The vaccine was given to people in several African countries. It reduced malaria by nearly 40 percent. The WHO continues to study this vaccine today to make sure it is safe. The vaccine may be made widely available in the future after further studies.

In 2016 more than 90 percent of malaria cases were in southern Africa. The hot weather there allows mosquitoes to transmit malaria all year long. Mosquitoes that carry the deadliest form of malaria parasite live in this area. Widespread poverty in Africa makes it difficult to treat and prevent malaria. But the new vaccine is giving many people hope.

vaccine—a substance made up of dead, weakened, or living organisms that is injected into a person to protect against a disease

Increased funding for malaria research and treatment has cut the malaria death rate by nearly half within the last decade. Scientists are once again hopeful that they can win the battle against malaria. The WHO has set a new goal of eliminating the disease worldwide by 2030. In 2018 Nigerian author Chimamanda Ngozi Adichie spoke about the global fight against malaria at the London Malaria Summit. She said, "We have the science and the knowledge to beat malaria. It is doable. May we also have the will to do it."

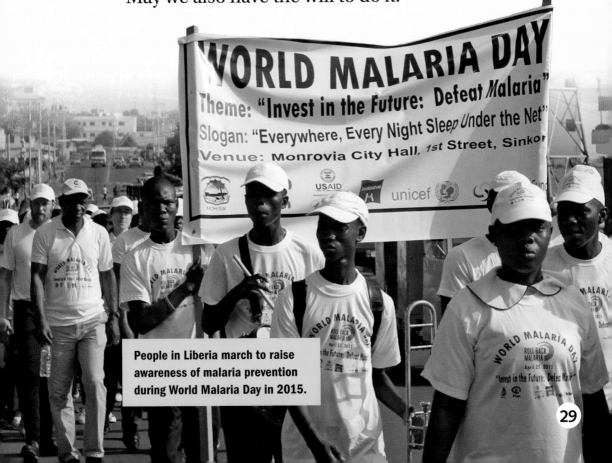

People in Liberia march to raise awareness of malaria prevention during World Malaria Day in 2015.

GLOSSARY

autopsy (AH-tahp-see)—an examination of a dead person's body that helps determine the cause of death

diagnose (dy-ig-NOHS)—to find the cause of a problem

epidemic (eh-pih-DEH-mik)—an outbreak of a disease that affects many people within a particular region

eradicate (eh-RAH-dih-kate)—to completely eliminate something, such as a disease

gene (JEEN)—the part of a cell that controls the traits passed down from parents to their children

organism (OR-gah-nih-zum)—a living thing that is made up of one or more cells

parasite (PAIR-uh-site)—a living thing that lives off another living thing, such as an animal or human

resistant (ri-ZIS-tuhnt)—no longer affected by a chemical or a drug

symptom (SIM-tuhm)—a change in a person's body or mind that is a sign of a disease

theory (THEER-ee)—an idea or set of ideas that scientists use to explain something

transmit (tranz-MIT)—to pass on something from one person to another

tropical (TRAH-pih-kuhl)—having a hot and humid climate

vaccine (vak-SEEN)—a substance made up of dead, weakened, or living organisms that is injected into a person to protect against a disease

READ MORE

Asselin, Kristine Carlson. *Dangerous Diseases: Scary Illnesses that Frighten the World.* Scary Science. North Mankato, Minn.: Capstone Press, 2014.

Donaldson, Olivia. *Malaria.* Deadliest Diseases of All Time. New York: Cavendish Square, 2015.

Hunt, Santana. *Bloodsucking Mosquitoes.* Real-Life Vampires. New York: Gareth Stevens, 2016.

INTERNET SITES

Use FactHound to find Internet sites related to this book.

Visit www.facthound.com

Just type in 9781543555059 and go.

Check out projects, games and lots more at
www.capstonekids.com

INDEX